<u>Preface</u>: Regardless of h̲ fellow human beings, there are now 8 billion of us. Earth's resources, especially drinking water, are limited and not sufficiently available to everyone. Most people agree that the population rate needs to slow dramatically. For now, all we can really do to stay sane is make observations about the overall human condition and find it amusing, sobering or downright bewildering. There seems to be no end to human suffering, cruelty, or the hideous tug-of-war between dominance and submission. In our quest to survive, it would be easy to give up hope in the face of this harsh reality. Because of this dilemma, it might be helpful to think of our current station in life as being stuck in a mid-evolutionary conundrum. In an attempt to offer up a lighter side of the human condition without 'ribbing' anyone but Calvin Jenkins and a few other imaginary characters, and with empathy for all, "The Great Disconnect" is the result of the Author's attempt to understand how we have become "disconnected" in so many ways. We put animals in cages, text instead of talk, wage war instead of peace, stare at our cell phones and spend billions of dollars trying to escape to the stars instead of maintaining fragile ecosystems here on Earth.

Chapter 1
The Adventure Begins

It all started late one August night in '56 in a small two-bedroom house in Overland Park, Kansas, when Calvin's Mother, Carol, decided that his older brother Chris needed a sibling. Chris was almost two at the time and Carol was hoping that a new baby would help to keep Chris occupied. Having been totally unaware of these deliberations, early embryonic consciousness came as a bit of a surprise to Calvin. After a few months of being upside down a lot, he came to the unique awareness that it was getting to be a tight squeeze. At around four months, he was ready to be let out. He felt that he could deal with the mid 1950's, but he had to wait for his legs and arms to grow into presentable proportions with his head. The months passed by in a series of spine popping growths. After eight months Calvin was aware of some upcoming transition, something that would dignify the reason for having had to endure the oftentimes distressful condition of being wet, upside down, toothless and without vision. Then, as if he were only going to be able to hold his breath for a couple more hours, he started trying to escape and ever the more frantic he became. After one such frenzied thrash, he heard Carol scream, which woke up his Dad, Jim. Carol exclaimed that Calvin kicked so hard that it knocked a bowl of ice cream off her TV tray. With that, Jim could be heard rustling his clothes on as he insisted that they go to the hospital. Once there, Calvin could feel himself rolling headlong down the smooth corridors toward the delivery room. He felt an ominous pressure coming from the area around his feet. He was ejected into the hands of someone who insisted on dangling him from his ankles. Breathing was a welcome relief. That was the spring of 1957. Although he couldn't relate to the historic significance of the baby boom officially peaking that year, Calvin could confirm that the maternity ward was a maddening cacophony of cries for attention. Five days in a hospital, and they were off to the suburbs of Overland Park. Calvin's eyes opened for the first time during the drive home. What he saw must have been the same as a dream considering he hadn't been conditioned to view the world a certain way yet. Looking up at Carol from the front seat was a sight for new eyes. He saw her turning some knobs and hearing a lot of different voices talking and singing. One guy kept yelling, "Good Golly, Miss Molly."

For all he knew, Calvin passed out for a few months because all of a sudden everybody decided it was his birthday. At last, he was one. He wasn't much of a partier, but to humor the revelers in attendance, he let them put a cone on his head that was secured by a rubber band under his chin. He was trapped in a chair by a food tray while they flashed camera bulbs in his direction. The bulbs would get so hot and melted that Jim had to wait a few minutes between pictures to reload with a fresh bulb.

At this point, Calvin drifted off and went in and out of sleep for a couple years. By the winter of 1960, the family had moved to a bigger house with a second floor. His parents got him and his brother a few matching presents that Christmas. There were the two stuffed Casper the Friendly Ghost's that were as big as they were. The Caspers had plastic white cowboy hats stapled to their heads. Of course, Calvin and Chris were compelled to take the staples out of the hats to wear themselves. The hats were a perfect fit. The boys soon discovered the Caspers true purpose. Up the stairs they'd go, laughing all the way, then toss the Caspers down the steps. The hatless ghosts would topple gracefully to the bottom of the stairs. This went on and on until the ghosts' heads started to detach. Carol had to toss them out after a couple of rough months. One day in mid-April, Carol came home and her over-sized stomach was gone, but in its place, she brought with her a new little brother, Terry. Now, with *two* brothers, a lot happened at that house over the next couple of years. The house looked like a barn from the outside. The front yard sloped downhill, but the backyard was flat and big enough for neighborhood baseball games. One time Calvin got into the family car and managed to shift the gears into neutral. The green '53 Chevy rolled down the hill, across the street, and into the neighbor's yard. Strike one for Calvin.

Calvin's next door neighbor, David, had a tree swing in his back yard. Shortly after take off from the top of a picnic table, Calvin would whiz past the tree trunk a little too close for comfort. He would have to kick the tree trunk with his scuffed saddle shoes to keep the trajectory straight.

Other days during the summer of 1962, He remembered listening to David's new transistor radio playing "Duke of Earl", "Wipe Out", and "Surfin' Safari" over and over. That's the year when Calvin learned how to test a 9-Volt battery by short circuiting it on his tongue. It's also the same year that he learned to not stick sewing needles into the electrical outlet.

Calvin had a pet turtle and kept it in a box in the back yard. He fed it lettuce and made sure it had water. He found out that keeping the turtle outside was not a good idea. One morning he went out to the backyard to visit his turtle. All that was left was the shell. He couldn't figure out how the turtle left its' shell and got out of the box. Jim had to break the bad news that turtles are permanently attached to their shells and that a raccoon had probably dug him out. Calvin gave the shell a proper burial and thought it best to mark the site by making a cross out of Popsicle sticks.

That same summer, Calvin and Chris were playing with golf balls and a baseball bat. Jim was focused on starting a fire on the charcoal grill just outside the back door and wasn't thinking of the potential hazard of the boys actions. Calvin had trouble holding up the heavy wooden bat, so it would be quite a feat if he hit the ball. What ensued haunted him for years. Carol had just come through the back screen door with a plate full of raw hamburger patties for the grill. At that precise moment, Chris pitched Calvin a golf ball and he managed to hit it squarely with the bat. The ball was a line drive that hit Carol right in the forehead. It all seemed like slow motion to Calvin. Carol fell backwards toward the door as the plate full of burgers flew off the plate into oblivion. Jim tried to catch Mom's fall as he saw the plate disintegrate. He remembered running to the front of their neighbor's house and hiding under their car. He wasn't sure what to do. He hid under the car for what seemed like an eternity. He could hear them call his name, but little Calvin was petrified. He finally came out and, of course, they forgave him. Carol was okay other than a big knot on her head. Strike two for Calvin.

In the summer of 1964 during a hailstorm, golf ball sized hail pelted the familys' green '53 Chevy as Carol and Calvin sat in the car in the driveway of their third, and last, house in Kansas. The car ended up resembling a giant green golf ball with dings, dents and a cracked windshield. Jim traded it in for a '62 VW bus.

Having assembled Calvin, Chris, Terry, Missy and Sally next to their Mother, Jim took a couple pictures of them in front of their house which was situated only two hundred feet from the old Santa Fe Trail. Jim got a new job in Ohio selling textiles, and the family was getting ready to move. It was late summer in 1965. The '62 VW bus that would transport them waited patiently for all seven of them to get 'all aboard' to tax its mechanisms. They queued up and squeakily boarded for a distant and mysterious destination. Chris and Calvin were the only two kids old enough to have any clue as to what was happening. So with that, they set out in their VW bus. They headed out on the trail as they left Shawnee Mission, Kansas.
Coursing along I-70, Chris and Calvin sat in the back playing 'Travel Bingo' and a battery operated Poker game. The family stayed overnight at a hotel in Effingham, Illinois that had a giant spiraling slide in the shape of a rocket ship and also a swimming pool. By the time they hit Dayton, Ohio, Jim announced that their destination loomed just 15 miles up the road. The glittering whites of the kids eyes peered across the landscape in search of that magical something one expects at the end of a long mysterious journey, and with the passing of those last minutes came the exit for Tipp City, Ohio.

Their first winter in Tipp City was the winter of '65-'66. They were renting the house of a judge who was going to be away for a few years working on an advanced degree. It was a 5-bedroom, 3-bath house. It only had a 1-car garage, which Carol was using to run a Dayton Daily News distribution hub for Tipp City. Even though Calvin was only 8 years old, and Chris only 10, they had their own paper routes. There were five other boys who would come there to get their papers which were delivered in bundles by box truck early afternoon Monday through Saturday, and at about 5a.m. on Sundays. One snowy, frigid, Sunday morning at about 6a.m., there were a couple inches of snow and it was about 20 degrees out. Calvin had to insert all the funny papers and advertisements into the giant newspaper, then load the papers into a saddlebag that went over the banana seat of his bike. The Sunday papers were 2 inches thick. He started out carefully pedaling and could feel the metal banana seat supports twisting and torquing from the weight of the papers. At one point the canvas saddlebag was hitting the wheel spokes and Calvin had to dismount and put the kickstand down to make some adjustments. The kickstand jammed into the snow and the bike fell over. It was too heavy to pick up, so Calvin had to take all the papers out, put them on the ground, pick the bike back up, and carefully reload the saddlebag with papers. Back then, you had to walk onto the porch, carefully place the paper between the customer's storm door and main front entry door in order be successful at the job. He couldn't get all 35 papers in the saddlebag, so he would have to come back to the garage, have a cup of hot chocolate and get a 2nd load of papers. He learned a lot about Physics that morning. He was determined and was able to finish his paper route.

Early one Saturday morning in the summer of '67, Calvin went down to the football field just for something to do. He was at the visitors side of the field at the far North end and noticed the remnants of a pole vaulting pit. Deeply imbedded into the grass and almost swallowed by the earth, was an old pole vault pole made from hollow aluminum, tapered at both ends. He pried it out of the ground. It must have been there since the 1940's, he was guessing. He picked it up to see how much it weighed. It seemed like it would be a little heavy to run with, but then Calvin only weighed about 95 pounds at the time. It made an impression on him and he thought that he might like to try pole vaulting someday. Then he went over to the home team side and went under the bleachers thinking he might find some coins that fell out of peoples pockets during the football games. Sure enough, he was finding all kinds of loose change. It seemed like a lot at the time, but it probably only amounted to a few dollars.

In the Summer of '68, Calvin's last year of playing Little League Baseball for West Main Barber Shop, he was selected to be on the All-Star team and now had a batting coach who helped Calvin a lot. His team won the championship in a late-night double-header against neighboring Piqua. Calvin finally hit a home run.

From 1966 to 1974, every 4th of July in Tipp City brought a Carnival group from some far out land. They set up for a 3-day stint in the City Park. The attractions were the Swings that would fling you out sideways, the metal egg that would be stopped when you were upside-down so that all the change would fall out of your pockets, a Bounce

House for kids, the device where you had to hit one side of a fulcrum with a sledge hammer that sent a chunk of metal up a rail in hopes that it would ring the bell which was affixed about 12 feet up, the Centrifugal Blood Coagulator that spun you around until all your blood was pooled in the back half of your body, a Bingo tent, and a .22 caliber Rifle Target Range to shoot metal ducks.

One of the Carnival family members, a boy of about 15, was trying to pick Calvin's pocket in the summer of '69 as he was standing in front of the game where you try to 'stand up' a 20 oz. bottle of ancient Canada Dry Jamaica Cola using a fishing pole with a 2" wooden ring at the end of the string. Calvin whipped around and caught the pick-pocket red-handed. It was all he could do to not punch the Carny creep in the stomach, but he restrained himself and simply warned the thief to never try that again. Calvin was only 12 years old, but he recognized the kid from previous years, as the Carnival family was the same every year. Calvin did win one bottle of the cola and opened it immediately but, to his dismay, it was void of carbonation. He gave it back to the carnival worker and suggested that they might want to order a fresh supply.

Jim was down at the dunking machine where you throw a baseball and try to hit a 5" round metal plate that is attached to a lever. If you hit the round plate, that would cause a latch to release and then the person who is perched on a seat falls abruptly into a 4 foot deep tank of cold water. Jim had volunteered to be the 'dunkee', having been a little league baseball coach, Cub Scout leader, and City councilman. Jim made a great target. Calvin took a few throws and was successful at dunking good old Dad. Jim was a good sport about it.

In Calvin's sophomore year, in the spring of '73, he decided to go out for the Track Team, having been on the Golf Team the year before. The High School still had an old cinder track and the runners had to wear ½" long cleats to get traction. It was pretty cold in the beginning of the season. Calvin started running low and high hurdles. The hurdles had counter weights so they wouldn't blow over. The problem was that they were *so* heavy they wouldn't fall over very easily if you should happen to hit one with your trail leg. There were several occasions when Calvins ankle hit the wood. It was an excruciating pain followed by a rush of endorphin. One time he lost his balance and had to break his fall with his hands in the cinders. Hurdles were getting old Calvin thought as he attended to his wounds. He also tried high jump and cleared 5'4" at one point, but there were already two guys, Benji and Phil, both of whom were 5'9" tall, but could scissors jump over 6'2". It was an amazing thing to watch. Then there was Larry the pole vaulter. Calvin was watching Larry one day and Larry was going over 7'6". It occurred to Calvin that Dick Fosbury, inventor of the 'Fosbury flop', had the world high jump record which was about the same height, and it inspired Calvin to give pole vaulting a try. The first day he tried out for pole vault, he asked Larry if he could use the pole. Calvin tried 6' and made it over. It seemed that the landing pit, which consisted of a fishing net full of big sponges, wasn't really adequate to land in from much higher up. Then he cleared 7', and then 8'. When he made it over 9', the coach came over and congratulated Calvin for making the team. No more running hurdles. Now

Calvin was going over a much higher hurdle with the help of a fiberglass pole. By the time the team went to the league track meet, he was able to consistently clear 11'. At that meet, he was attempting 11'6" and didn't have enough momentum going into the vault. He stalled directly over the metal box where you plant the pole, dropped straight down 11'6" onto his back in the box. He was temporarily paralyzed. Eventually, Jim and Carol drove the family station wagon around to the pole vault pit, folded down the back seats and loaded Calvin into the wagon on his back and took him home.

The next spring, after having recovered, the school bought Calvin a new fiberglass pole. He was clearing 12' on a regular basis now and was doing well in the regular track meets. On the first day of the Southwest Buckeye League track meet, which consisted of 10 teams, he was one of the last three contenders, and it was already dark and starting to rain. All three of the finalists had cleared 12'. Calvin had to use a lot of special adhesive spray to keep a grip on the pole in the steady rain. When the bar went up to 12'6", all three of them had missed their 2nd attempts. The two guys from Northridge High then missed their 3rd attempts. On Calvin's 3rd try, he took off down the runway, got a good plant into the box, went over the bar and barely brushed it with his stomach. As he fell into the pit, he looked up to see the crossbar moving ever so slightly. It stayed up and he got out of the pit, clinching first place.

One summer morning in '72, when Calvin was 15, Carol drove him eight miles to his job at a restaurant in Troy, Ohio where he worked in the kitchen as a prep cook on weekdays, portioning Alaskan King Crab legs, and

working 12 hour shifts on weekends cleaning up until
1a.m. hosing down the floor mats and washing pots. One
weekday shift when his work was finished at about 4p.m.,
he headed home in his bib overalls, walking toward the
railroad tracks about a block from the restaurant. He heard
a freight train coming and started thinking he might hop
on, knowing it might get him to Tipp City. The train was
going slow enough, so he ran alongside, grabbed a rung of
a cars ladder and hopped on. The drivers of the
automobiles that were stopped at the railroad crossing
were scratching their heads observing Calvin, imagining
how his adventure might play out.
When the train was about halfway to Tipp City, and as
they were going around a bend along the Miami River,
Calvin stuck his head out from between the cars to take a
look. The man in the caboose saw Calvin and alerted the
Engineer to stop the train. When the train came to a halt,
Calvin saw the brake man heading his way, so he jumped
off and headed full speed toward the river, looking for a
place to cross. He waded chest deep and made it across
the river, ending up in a high cornfield, heart pounding.
He ran and ran, not knowing where he would end up. He
came out to an open field where there was some rusty farm
machinery. He heard faint voices and made his way to a
barn where people were buying cantaloupes and corn.
Since overalls take a while to dry, he was still a little
soaked. He asked an elderly couple if they were by any
chance going to Tipp City. They said 'yes' and that they
would give Calvin a ride, never inquiring about his
saturated condition. The couple stopped at their house
which happened to be next door to Calvin's friend Matt's
house, and only a block from his own house. He then told
them that he used to deliver their Dayton Daily newspapers

when he was 9 or 10. He thanked them and headed home, surprised at the adventure a day can deliver.

In August of 1975, the summer Calvin graduated High School, he and friends Matt, Benji, Lee, Charlie and Steve went out to Ludlow Falls to jump off the waterfall and maybe the bridge. They were all going off the waterfall at around 15 feet up. The bridge was 63 feet. Having grown up diving from the 10 foot springboard every summer, Calvin was the only one considering going off the bridge. He decided he might give it a try, so he swam out to where he thought he might enter the water and sank down as deep as he could to see if he could touch bottom. The water was very murky and he could not see under water. His feet did not touch bottom at what he figured to be 12 to 15 feet. He had no idea how deep he would go from a 63 feet dive, but he went up on to the bridge to see if he wanted to try it. A local kid about his age said he had jumped off before, so Calvin told the local boy that he would go off if the local went first. The local kid jumped and landed awkwardly on his left side. He smacked pretty hard and swam to the rocks at the waters edge to recuperate. Calvin climbed over the railing and his heart started racing as he gathered up some courage. He didn't want to enter feet first, thinking that would be too dangerous. He always preferred entering the water head first. He knew how to do a proper dive to keep control. He also knew how to clasp his hands at entry so as to not break his neck. There were a lot of people there and it was to be a first that anyone knew of for someone to dive head first from the bridge. Calvin took a few deep breaths, then launched out horizontally as far from the bridge as possible in order to clear the waterfalls below. He was basically flying for about 2 to 3 seconds at about 45 m.p.h. as he kept his back, neck, and head arched, and his arms spread straight out until it was time for entry. He punched through the surface very fast and when he slowed to a stop underwater at about 15 feet down, his fingers on his right hand touched mud. It didn't occur to him how lucky he was that he didn't break his neck on the bottom. He was more concerned with finding the surface as he couldn't see a foot in front of his face and was disoriented and out of breath because his heart was pounding out of his chest. He reached the surface just as he was going to have to inhale something, regardless of whether it was air or water. What a relief that was. He swam to the rocks where the local kid was. The kid's whole left side was red and tiny drops of blood could be seen at a lot of the pores on his skin. He didn't look too happy. Calvin felt like he had just been squeezed through a tube of toothpaste. His chest muscles felt like they were about to detach from his rib cage. He climbed back up to the bridge thinking that the dive wasn't too bad and that he might do a 1-1/2 the next dive. He thought about how slowly he would have to rotate so as to not land on his back. He launched out and started the flip. As he completed a full flip and was getting prepared to enter the water, he could tell he was going to rotate over a little too far. He entered, not on his back, but it was close. He tumbled through the darkness, totally disoriented and not knowing in which direction to swim to get to the surface. Again, he lucked out and made it out just in time. As he climbed up to the waterfall level, a couple stopped him and said they had taken a picture of the dive. Calvin gave them his address and he received the picture in the mail a week later.

A couple of weeks after the Ludlow Falls dive, it was time for Calvin to pack up and get ready for the trip to the coast of Oregon and a year at Millard School. While he was to be gone, the family was also going to pack up and move to Cincinnati, about 70 miles South of Tipp City. Calvin's girlfriend drove to his house to say goodbye. She would be going to Ohio State University. Calvin was waiting for her on the front porch. He had been attracted to her since he first saw her in 3rd grade just after arriving in Tipp City in 1965. They were very close and it was going to be very painful to say goodbye. As she walked up the stairs, Calvin couldn't hide his profound sadness. His throat seized up with a great sorrow to where he could scarcely even breathe. He was unable to speak. His anguish sufficed in conveying the gravity of that moment. He embraced her, wishing it could be forever, at the same time accepting that it was probably *over* forever.

Chapter 2
The Last Traveling Encyclopedia Salesman

A freezing late November wind chilled the lines in Calvin's face as he walked the last mile toward the outskirts of Greenfield, Massachusetts to get his VW bus that had just been repaired. Having moved to New England, he had driven through the hills selling Encyclopedias for thirteen years since he graduated from High School in 1975. He got mixed reviews from his teachers, having not been a very serious student. His favorite course was on Philosophers and Mathematicians like Plato and Pythagoras. He kept that textbook with him after graduation and referred to it often. The numbing centrifuge of life, along with a preconceived notion of his innate limitations, ingrained Calvin with a humble demeanor. He felt that the purpose of life was to *find a purpose,* then just keep moving forward. In school he learned about how our planet took a funny bounce eons ago, causing a wobble that facilitated our having the four seasons and biological life. Now here *we* are. The futility of excessive striving did not appeal to him because he saw humans tripping over one another in competitive ways only to end up at the back of the line. He preferred keeping to himself when he wasn't working and tried to balance the seriousness of life and what he felt was a comical side of the human condition.

Calvin saw the momentum of life as a behemoth destiny bulldozing ahead, while humanity represented a defiant predator roosting, an unflinching apex entity bent on ego boosting. A plague of bad behavior by narcissistic world leaders was causing a lot of human suffering, and the cacophony of rage in the world was getting louder. The human race was in a mid-evolutionary conundrum of shallow thinking. How can humans survive if all they do is bicker? *Perceived* injustices only made things worse. He had to question what some called "progress." In a society that seemed to be in retrograde, each day seemed like another race to the starting line.

As he continued to wheel his way from town to town over the years, he became more appreciative of his surroundings. Living in the country and being able to see deer, hawks, and wild turkeys was important. He had no interest in guns or hunting. The concept of superiority and the subduing of the weak made no sense to him.

His greatest hope was that the whole world would wake up and realize that people have been heading for disaster since the invention of the Atom Bomb and that the road to ruin is well paved with ill intentions. "Ignorance may be bliss, but stupidity isn't so forgivable" was one of the lines he liked to use. The masses would have to get smarter and work together in order to get through the challenges that were heading their way.

When Calvin first started selling Encyclopedias, he might ask his customer where they were on the spectrum of religious devotion. Whether they were religious, believed in Evolution, or even the Buddhist philosophy, whose adherents do not believe in a

17

supreme creator, Calvin would mention that religious stories from books that are thousands of years old, or translated into other languages, had details that were distorted or lost in the translation. Poorly assembled words had set humanity back farther than innumerable silences and plainly spoken fact. He wasn't successful at closing a sale with highly evangelized people who fell back on the idea that Deities controlled everything. Their belief systems seemed to be in conflict with a lot of the scientific information that was in the Encyclopedias.

Calvin was most successful selling to open minded people. One day he called on a couple who had become disillusioned with their Church. They felt that people were being strung along by religions that talked about the afterlife in the same breath that they were asking for money. The wife thought that religions caused way too much alienation and conflict and that few religious scholars had come up with ideas to solve this dilemma. She felt that reducing the number of religions might be a good start. It made no sense to them that, just because someone might not pray enough, they can't get into Heaven. They had both concluded that even if there were a Heaven, it would be some kind of dysfunctional political system.

When Calvin turned thirty-one in 1988, and technology started to take over the printing business, hard copy Encyclopedias were becoming obsolete, and he became a bit despondent. In his leisure, he read Science Fiction, and sometimes imagined it as fact. Calvin thought that, at some point, technology will have outlived its usefulness. He was sure that there were life forms out there that *must* be smarter than us. To them, *we* are the aliens. It seemed that the human race was stuck midway between the past and someplace not reachable by any stretch of the imagination. In the future, digital souls would waft through the Universe as ill-spent "ones" and "zeros."

He imagined that the day might come when the human race would be thought of as an unwanted guest on Earth that never met their potential and wore out the "Welcome Mat" going about the business of polluting the planet.

These thoughts were flooding his mind now since the ebb of his career. Although he continued to try and sell, he had come to an uneasy truce with his ambitions and felt that the end was near. Earthly bonds, looser now, made way for some transitions.

Calvin felt that he was being reeled in by the stars, but was grateful and in awe of the fact that he was hanging out on the only inhabitable planet within humanities grasp.

One day he stopped to eat his lunch at an old graveyard called Hope Lawn Cemetery. There was a bench for him to sit on. He wondered where they came up with the name "Hope Lawn". He walked around reading all the epitaphs. Engraved on the last tombstone in one of the rows it said, "I made it safely to my grave, now I get to rest." As he was getting ready to leave, a gust of wind snapped off a tree branch that hit him squarely on the top of his head. His vision became blurred. He touched his head and looked at his hand. There was a lot of blood and he could sense that it might be serious, but didn't panic because he was already at a cemetery. Getting delirious, Calvin started having colorful and amusing hallucinations. He felt as if he were being joined by a fortress of onlookers and other affiliates of the afterlife banging pots with spoons. He envisioned old gunslingers like Slim Chances and Quiet Earp, swashbuckling grannies in combat boots, the Dwindling Lineage Singers and a banjo playing cat. He felt a great sense of calm as these characters rallied around him. Calvin laid back, eyes up to the sky, seeing beyond the falling leaves through the filtered sunlight. Twenty minutes later, he regained full consciousness and his hallucinations dissipated. Feeling clear headed enough to get back on his feet, he got up and walked over to his bus and drove toward home with a renewed sense of purpose.

When Calvin got home, he reviewed his written collection of phrases, one-liners, and story ideas. He then started arranging them into a Sci-Fi story called "The Great Disconnect".

Chapter 3
The Great Disconnect

Calvin moved South in 1995, settled in Florida, and got a job as a Purchasing Manager at a plastics factory. He bought a small house, got married and had a stable life, but nothing could have prepared him for what happened one day while jogging on Juno Beach. It was a beautiful August Sunday afternoon. The beach was sporting its usual variety of visitors...fisherman, swimmers, surfers, and families. He ran the first two miles. On the return trip of two miles, he decided to walk, space out, and look at the Ocean. There was a storm brewing far offshore. He heard the long low rumble of thunder in the distance, and the strangest thing occurred to him. As he glanced around, he noticed the absence of people where he thought he should see some. Fishing gear was left unattended. Blankets with coolers, children's toys and items of clothing were left on the sand. There were still people around, but not as many. There were no children at all. The people who were left seemed to be sharing in the same observations. He could hear one man, just ahead, calling out for someone. As Calvin approached, the man asked Calvin if he had seen a 4-year old boy carrying an orange plastic pail.

"I wasn't paying any particular attention earlier when I was running. But it does seem as if the beach emptied out all of a sudden. Where is everyone?"

"I don't know, but this is freaking me out!"

The man ran to the shore and was looking around for any sign of his son.

"He was right near me a few minutes ago while I was checking my fishing line, and then I looked around and there was no sign of him. I think I would have seen him if he had gone in the water."

"Maybe he went to your car, said Calvin."

"Yea, can you come with me? Maybe you'll spot him."

"What is your name?"

"Jake…yours?"

"I'm Calvin."

Jake pointed out to sea, "There's a huge cargo ship out on the horizon."

"Yes, I can see it out there where the storm is brewing."

"Are you thinking what I'm thinking?"

"That the ship has something to do with your son disappearing?"

"Maybe, but I'm probably just imagining things. It looks surreal the way the ship is lingering in the middle of the lightening storm."

"Something weird is going on, that's for sure."

"Let's run up to my car to see if my son is up there."

Calvin and Jake both ran up the 20 or so steps to A1A. When they got to the sidewalk and looked out onto the street, it was almost devoid of people, but there were cars parked in the middle of the street with the doors open.

"It seems likely that some bizarre disconnect has taken place. People don't just leave their cars in the middle of the street."

Jake checked his car and there was no sign of the boy.

"It seems obvious to me that this abduction, disconnect, or whatever you want to call it, is meant to somehow protect the innocent people. I have to assume for now that my son is safe. I wonder what I did that they left me here?"

"Maybe nothing. Maybe some of us who are left here have another purpose."

"Maybe we're wearing out our welcome on Earth."

"Not enough people know the Golden Rule, that's for sure. Without that, how do they expect to progress as a species?"

"Few people are willing to take responsibility for their mistakes. They'd rather try and save face."

"If there's a God, I wish he'd show up."

"I don't think he wants to be known and I can't think of too many good reasons that he would want to know us. We've messed up the planet he gave us. We took a perfectly good planet and pretty much ruined it. The sad part is that it is being ruined on purpose. Earth doesn't need *us* breaking things constantly. God might have taken a permanent glance at our plight, stepped on the gas, and kept going. I'm sure he has plenty of other things to do."

"I think he would respect us more if we had a 'healthy disregard' for *him*. He doesn't need *us* somehow thinking we've got him all figured out."

"All I know is that we were given plenty of chances to take care of this planet."

"The cell phones aren't working. I am going to run home to see if my wife is there. I'll see if I can report your son's disappearance at the Police Station. There should still be some police around."

"No rush. Time has become irrelevant."

"I heard that."

On the way home, a full-blown memory came to Calvin's mind. He felt that he had dreamt this scenario when he was very young. Abandoned cars were everywhere. The people that were left driving around were either panicking or appeared dazed and bewildered. Many were on cell phones, unable to contact anyone. Elsewhere in the world, prison guards were sounding alarms thinking that prisoners had escaped. Disorganized television broadcasts reported that there was a lot of looting.

Calvin got home and his wife wasn't there. He was prepared for that. He presumed she was safe, so he was off to report Jake's son missing and then back to the beach to see if he could be of any help. Calvin met back up with Jake.

"It seems this mystery entity pulled the plug on humanity by removing all the innocent people and letting the rest of us work things out down here."

"It seems logical that there can only be one Creator, but there could also be an advanced extraterrestrial entity from another solar system messing with us."

"It kind of seems that way. I was just thinking that we need to get honest with ourselves. If people refuse to acknowledge their flaws, we contribute to the detriment of all species. We've got to engineer the reverse of global warming. We can't just keep kicking the can down the road."

"We're all going to kick the *bucket* down the road sooner than later if we don't fix this. Most people don't want to believe that we are just another animal species. That would be too big of a leap for a lot of us. It's a mental block that is keeping us from being able to progress as a species."

"Humans took a fatal diversion from the natural world. Since the invention of the wheel, stone tools, and spears, man keeps making machines of unending complexity.

With each new invention or supposed 'advancement' it seems we are just digging a deeper hole for ourselves."

"People think that just because they talk and drive cars around, they are somehow special among the other life forms on the planet. We are barely smarter than apes, and far from being comparable to the smartest beings in the Galaxy."

"There is a distorted anachronism playing out because of our infatuation with the past. The reason we dwell on the past is because it seems closer and more real than the future. We *should* be more focused on the present and the future."

"We've gone too far in whatever direction it is that we think we're going."

"And the endless cycle of people thinking they are going to solve all the world's problem's is not based in reality. The wheel can only be reinvented so many times until it's worn out."

"We are the poster child for the "not likely to survive" competition. Over-thinking, twisted egos, and living in the past seems to be the norm. It should be the opposite; where we keep things simple, stay humble, and *progress* into the future."

"Humans didn't exist for billions of years. We've only been around for 300,000 years or so, and will probably become extinct at some point. In a sense, we can't really blame ourselves. We are stuck in a mid-evolutionary conundrum. We all want to see the good side of humanity, but that's getting more difficult by the day."

"People can't do two things at once. I saw a kid almost get hit crossing the street while he was looking at his cell phone. People have even fallen into the Grand Canyon taking selfies. Conflicting necessities are another puzzle. We want to think we are special, yet we dislike other people who think that they are special. We choose our poison based upon some faction's ideals, all of which are based on suspect motives. Humans are flawed based simply on past performance and how unwilling or unable we are to learn from the past."

"The frustration that the human race endures won't stop for one simple reason. The human ego is unique, complicated, and no one seems to know how to stop the confusion that people experience. Eckhart Tolle wrote the book, "A New Earth", in the 1990's. It's a guide for people to learn how to free themselves from the bondage of the ego."

"We won't be able to do *anything* about our decline until we stop our habit of burning everything we see that's made of carbon."

Calvin and Jake looked at each other and realized it was time to take a break from their philosophical meanderings. Calvin could see the look on Jake's face. He was distraught over his son's disappearance. They drank a few sodas that were in a cooler in Calvin's trunk.

"I find it really strange that whales were hunted almost to extinction. How could it have not been obvious to the owner's of the whaling ships that whales were intelligent and so advanced that they had also developed lungs."

"They just *had* to get that whale oil, and then more whale oil. People will never stop looking for an easier and softer way through life. Humans don't seem to ever be satisfied."

"True. Yet everybody's busy chasing their tails. We have nowhere else to go."

"Snorkeling in a fog through the swamps of life keeps us busy. In time, the swamp and fog become one."

"Cooperation in the world has to start somewhere. Maybe the abductors can get everybody on the same wave length. A good start would be to simply agree to disagree, without all the violence. Then, advance from there on an even footing."

"At this point, with wars, wildfires and CO2 pollution, the Earth is just spinning around getting fried."

"Mars is all that matters anymore. We are going to have to go to Mars because we have pretty much ruined Earth. Maybe the lack of human activity will allow the Earth to cool down. We have already left a bunch of trash on Mars. We will ruin Mars at some point and move on to mess up even more planets. Humans seem to specialize in planetary destruction."

"I hear what you're saying Jake, but Mars ain't broke, so we don't need to fix it. I think our money would be better spent *fixing* Earth rather than *breaking* Mars. We are just ingredients mixing with the infinite expanse, not masters of the bloody Universe, for God's sake! That's my self-assessment, but what the hell do I know? All that and a dime will get me a cup of coffee."

"People have the burden of thinking that they have to somehow consume all the excesses of materialism. Material possessions can only hold us down as long as we let them. We keep collecting all this 'stuff', a lot of which we don't even need."

"People should ask themselves the question, 'What am I doing and why am I doing it? It's a really simple question for complicated times."

"I may not be a genius, but at least I have the wherewithal to stay off Facebook, Twitter, and Instagram. Unlike some moronic politicians who keep tweeting their little temper tantrums. Some politicians attempt to glamorize and embellish their usefulness. Some of them are in a desperate race to be immortalized even if it is for nefarious activity."

"History for people has been a blood soaked struggle of one kind or another. I can't make sense of it. Sometimes it feels like whoever's in charge might be having second thoughts about creating people."

"I know this is going to sound like a stretch, but I have a theory that accommodates both evolution and religion. The Creators of human beings could have been extraterrestrials that happened to visit here about 200,000 years ago. They would have already mastered genetics.

When they saw that apes with 24 pairs of chromosomes could be 'improved' and made to walk upright, they would have been able to figure out that they could modify the apes chromosomes to 23 pairs, which is what humans have. Earth might be like a Petri dish for an advanced civilization to conduct experiments. They could have created 'Adam and Eve', the religious version, or Homo Habilis, the evolutionary version. My theory, if accepted would put everyone on the same page. Homo Habilis, and then Homo Erectus, walked upright and were the first human ancestors."

"You can believe in a Creator or not believe in one. The predicament is that, in a world without a Deity, there would be no one left to blame. Humans are reluctant to take the blame for anything. The Creator probably isn't that keen on religions. The Papacy would certainly appear ludicrous in the *absence* of a God. To keep my sanity, I have to believe in a higher power or something greater than myself. 'God' can simply be a defined moment within one's self. If all people acted in concert as one unified and peaceful body, we would actually be God."

"Religion was probably created, in part, as a safety net for those who can't handle the concept of a natural death."

"At the rate we're going, God may have lost interest in us."

"Maybe the human race has been so chaotic that the Creator had to make the difficult decision to watch us self destruct rather than intervene."

"It's probably not a great idea to wait until the last minute to reconcile with the Creator. It would be best for people to come to grips with their mortality whether they like the outcome, or not. People would be well served to quit praying on everything and be thankful for the good things that happen to them. People *claiming* that they know the Creator seems pretty whacked out to me."

"In my opinion, the word God is a good acronym for 'Good Orderly Direction' and that's about it. People have taken the 'God' thing way too far."

"Some people are incensed at the thought of having to suffer this life and there be no reward. Religion was born out of this dilemma."

"There are people who are assuming redemption. I think that would be insulting to any self-respecting Creator. Jesus doesn't want us bothering him about coming back to Earth. Why would he want to come back? We didn't treat him too well the last time he was here. He may not have enough faith left in us or he would help us straighten out the mess we are in. He already taught us what we need to know, but it went in one ear and out the other. Existence should be all about love and respect and nothing more, not about appeasing invisible Deities."

"We can help ourselves by helping each other. We can't all be 'number one'. So, it only follows that *nobody* can be 'number one'."

"The fading twilight of unattended brains is the human races' main deficit. We have become like old cars ditched by the side of life's long road. It seems like we're not evolving."

"Those of us that are still here need to get busy figuring out how to stop all the pollution. It's time to repair the damage that's been done."

"Petro-lunacy is the biggest elephant in the room and it has been for 100 years. The ignorance of oil gluttons is what has caused such bad behavior in humans and, as we know, ignorance feeds upon itself. Now one oil emergency replaces the next."

"I can imagine a day when there are a lot less people. The wild animals will fare a lot better, I'm sure."

"Some people get trapped in a game of manipulation, forever scheming and trying to outwit others. Some people race down the ladder to be in the lowest common denominator."

"The whole cycle of retribution and revenge leaves no room for the prospects of peace. That cycle needs to be broken before we can progress. The small minded people, who are convinced that their minds are large, disenfranchise all other life forms for a fleeting glimpse in the rear-view mirror as they primp and preen, then suddenly crash headlong off the precipice of their self-made gang-plank."

"When you kick the can of time down the road long enough, you end up with a Possum-Jack-Ass hybrid that runs the world. A creep that moves like a rat through a

New York City sewer and does nothing but lie, cheat, and steal his whole life. Who needs vain miscreants with vile protocols exalting their primal insecurity, lost in age-old beliefs?"

"The only way to get to the truth is to stop lying. I say, don't believe anything until it's true. It's been said that the truth will set you free; that the freed mind has no boundaries. When people tap the unlimited powers of their minds, they might find peace. We have suffered a long way through an infirmary of diabolic citizenry to a utopian backwash of useless sin. The road to ruin is scorched with ill intent."

"If fairness and being able to see both sides of an argument are admirable qualities, then why would we want to choose an affiliation with a particular political party? A good leader should never be disparaging, and always facilitate a solution. If our leaders have flown off the handle, then who's at the helm? Some so-called leaders have a need to pilfer. They have inculcated into their psyche how to divide and conquer. Divide rather than unify. They always have a puss on their face and hover over everyone like a turd in a fishbowl. Once a country is in the grips of a tyrant, it is like pulling out of Hell with the brakes on trying to get away from them. Their motto is, 'out wit, and out stupefy'. Their mentality toward the people is, 'You're just a bug'. All the mistaken assumptions, perpetuated through lack of information, leave the populace ignorant and vulnerable to the tyrant's base of miscreants. I can't venture a guess as to what those fools are thinking. Are they trying to build a kingdom or dig a grave?"

"Aspiring tyrants living in Democracies are a bunch of nuts with chips on their shoulders. Their blind followers twist their own thoughts to identify with the already familiar unreasonableness of their own lives. They ask for trouble, almost begging, and swallow what they are told, like the mindless idiots they always wanted to be."

"We would be well served to get our priorities straight. We could all slow down and pay more attention to the big picture instead of the overwhelming minutia of everyday life."

"How would you describe what a civilization is?"

"Ideally, I think that civilization would be a place where people have abandoned the practice of surreptitiously perpetrating horrendous stupidity upon one another."

"With that Jake, I gotta go. I'll be back here tomorrow."

"Okay. I will be back also."

The next day, they were listening to the radio. For the next two hours, reports indicated that a second wave of abductions was occurring. Several passenger jets had to make emergency landings after some pilots and crew members disappeared. It was estimated that a quarter of the world population had vanished.

Epilogue

All the missing people returned two weeks later. Jake raced back to the beach to look for his son. As he ran down the steps and onto the sand, the first thing that caught his eye was his little boy and the orange pail. The boy was playing in the sand. Jake could barely contain his emotions as he approached and called out to his son. The boy turned around and called out to Jake, oblivious to all that had taken place. Jake embraced his son. His heart was racing as he tried to hold back tears. The boy had returned to where he was last seen with no recollection of where he had been. The 'Earth-bound' population had become very well behaved, more humane, and normal as a result of the abduction. Enough time had passed for people all over the world to realize and agree that there was only one higher power. Most religions were abandoned and new philosophies were embraced. The human race breathed a collective sigh of relief. The return of the missing people brought humility to the Earth-bound who had finally gravitated away from their bad behavior and chaotic ways. It clarified the purpose for behaving well and living a good life. When family and friends rejoiced at the return of the missing, those returning were mystified by the warm reception. The Earth-bound, who had been rude or problematic in their own unique ways, seemed to have gained some wisdom and were now a joy to be around. They had been reintroduced to the ancient realization and belief that the cosmos matters, that our planet is fragile, and that we are all connected. It seemed the abductors knew how to get their message across. They had the ability to give and take to effectuate the continuation of the human species in a more progressive, less chaotic way. The world birth rate slowed over the next few years, as did the frequency of war. People came to realize that procreation could no longer be the casual consideration that it had once been. The great 'healing' that Calvin imagined had finally begun.

Authors note: In keeping with the theme of this book, Chapters 4 through 6 are completely "disconnected" from Chapters 1 through 3. Chapter 4 is comprised of 11 comical Vignettes that Calvin put together over the course of several years. Chapter 5 is comprised of some of Calvin's poetry. Chapter 6 consists of shorter euphemisms and one-liners.

Chapter 4
A Spoof on the Human Condition

Vignette 1

Clovis Bigglebee was standing outside a day-old bread store waiting for a sandwich to happen when he met his wife, Wanda. He was busily calculating Cyberkinetic morph ratios in his head at the time, and a compelling thought occurred to him. The first thing he asked Wanda was "which direction do you load a toilet paper roll?" When she said "overlap", he immediately asked her to marry him. It just so happens that she had on a "Yikes Super Bra", "Holy Mother of God Underwear", and "Sheer Nonsense Pantyhose" that day and was feeling very chipper. During previous courtships, most women Clovis dated would leave underwear or a toothbrush at his house, she left Tupperware. He found that odd, but endearing, and he told her so. Wanda was more than happy to shed her old maiden name, Wartwhacker. It had been a source of consternation her whole life. Clovis had always wanted to get married and now his wife was Wanda Bigglebee. He bought her a wedding "spring" instead of a ring so, if she got bigger, it would expand. Clovis had always made meager attempts to stay in shape. He burned most of his calories dusting off his exercise equipment.

Their neighbors and best friends, the Follinofski's, were descendants of one of those old West families who were named after what they did, like the Smiths or Carpenters. The Follinofski's were named because they kept falling off their horses. The Follinofski's, Fred and Fanny, didn't get along too well. Static cling was the only thing keeping them together. He had more money than he could burn and it caused some strife in the marriage. Fanny liked to pester Fred. To make light of her taunts whenever the Bigglebee's were there, Fred loved to say in jest, "The only way to fight a woman is with your hat…grab it and run!"

Vignette 2

The following summer, in the next town over from Brokenyoke, Arkansas, Carla Crumbcatcher, Condo "pool queen" from the Breakwind Condominiums, chaired the 'Rodent Awareness Weekend' opening ceremonies. When the residents weren't floating around in the pool with their water noodles, they would be minding someone else's business, or someone's dog's business. Rita Rubbernecker and her chihuahua Goober were out for a walk. Rita's head turned quickly to see if she were being watched, then she and Goober sped off after Goober did his business. You could hear Sara Bellum scream from the pool, "We saw that! Get your ass back here and pick that up!" Sara was the condo party girl and was usually looking for any reason to start celebrating. She was a little on the fried side. She's the buzz that was. She had a cut on her elbow that day and explained to her friends, "I cut myself putting the Band-Aids away." The irony escaped most of the attendees, as there was an abundance of alcoholic beverages being consumed, like the two new cocktails "Arctic Slush" and "Permafrost Daiquiri". Dental hygiene was not Sara's strong suit. She had drifted from barn dance to barn dance in recent years in search of a dance, but was most times left at the barn. Most of those in attendance at the pool started to lose interest when who showed up but Clovis Bigglebee from Brokenyoke. He hadn't been out of earshot of a chicken his whole life, so listening to the cackling of Carla, the condo queen made him feel right at home. Clovis got to talking with Ms. Crumbcatcher and they got on the subject of how there are entirely too many commercials on television nowadays. Clovis said that his hometown newscaster and weathergirl Donna Dewpoint did her last story on the evening news about how hemorrhoid and diarrhea commercials were outlawed in China during the dinner hour because people were losing their appetites. "The Chinese need all the nutrition they can get in order to maintain their trade surplus over the United States, you know." Donna spoke in a far out, ethereal way as if her thoughts were merely dreamt. Her mind was too big for Brokenyoke. The people there seemed small minded. She described the effect of living there as "plowshares of ignorance glancing sparks off dirtclods of intolerance." She knew that only a jackass would argue with another jackass and yet that was exactly what she experienced there. That was enough to make her want to move away. She gave them a piece of her mind, and now there was nothing left.

Vignette 3
That weekend, at the local hotel where out-of-town business visitors would usually stay, a suspicious unattended bag, who went by the name of

Density, sat in the lounge. She had just arrived from a trendy new boutique. She sported a remotely operated hairdo, all the rage at the time. She could push a button to make her bouffant slowly rise up, then push the button again to make it fall elegantly. She let her hair down at the bar. She had meant to put down some loose change, but she had much more hair than money. Cosgrove Hairpile, a local hairdresser witnessed the whole display and was immediately smitten with Density. Density's mother had wanted to name her "Destiny", but spelled it wrong. The name stuck. After several stiff drinks, Cosgrove and Density stumbled into the night. The bartender saw a roach scampering across the bar. He discretely squished it and the barmaid whispered, "What did you go and do that for, now 400 of his friends will come to bury him." A visitor from Dogslobber, Iowa had been in town a few days trying to get away from a problematic relationship, seeking sanctuary from the silence of sadness. He was using the newspaper to hide behind mostly, but having had no choice but to read the paper, noticed an ad for a new store, "Bedrash and Beyond" for people who could barely get out of bed, and the new shampoo called "Nogginwash". Miss America was on tour and happened to be in town for the day. A small group of reporters had gathered around her at the end of the bar and were asking her some questions. "Would you do anything to help crime?" Her response…"Yes, I always wanted to rob a bank." Another reporter asked her, "What would you do to help save the human race and planet Earth?" She said "No problem, we can eventually mold a new planet out of our landfill materials." Later that evening, a local entertainer was impersonating Katherine Hepburn doing a rendition of "Lucy in the Sky With Diamonds". The audience was spellbound by the performance. One patron who had consumed a large quantity of raw broccoli appetizers expelled gas in such a violent manner that it was thought to have altered the rotation of the earth slightly for several seconds. The impersonator stopped to catch his breath, but there was no oxygen left in the room and he passed out. Some local teenagers were driving past the bar on their way to Mount Runamuk and stopped about a half block down the street to pick up one of their buddies who was waiting for them. He was leaning up against his Dads gun case when the broccoli induced eruption occurred at the club. He fell into a pile of old army bullets. One of the bullets went off. Fortunately it was stopped by his wallet full of fake I.D's. Later up on Mount Runamuk the boys gazed at the stars pondering the true meaning of the days events. One of them concluded, "This town's like Jello. One wrong move and the whole world knows."

Vignette 4

The following Friday down at the "Wits End" bar a production company was filming an episode of the new soap opera, "As the Argument Weakens". Several of the cast were trying shots of a new liquor. The label on the bottle read "Dr. Spock Vodka…It'll make your ears point." The star of the show, Biff Starlow, came to a screeching halt outside the bar in his new Dodge "Hangover". He was running late and looked very disheveled. He had had an unsuccessful drinking career, so he took up acting a few years earlier. His day had not gone well so far. He had been stood up by a woman, and knocked down by a car. The night before he had visited the new bordello, 'Cleopatra's Mattress'. Another car screeched up behind Biff Starlow's. It was a lady they called Buffalo Betty in a late model Jaguar. She was a bit of a mess, but enjoyed low level luxury. She had just purchased an outfit from a clothing store called "The Fashion Hole." She was checking her look in the mirror. She had some fibrous mango residue in her teeth, a retired hairdo, and had apparently not been keeping up with her eyebrow maintenance program. She sounded like a combination of Bob Dylan, Ronald Reagan, and Floyd the Barber. She was a groupie who would tend to show up during filming, hoping to be an extra. She was always in a panic, but they loved her just the same.

Vignette 5

Meanwhile, at the board meeting taking place up in the administrative office of the "Fashion Hole", grandiose ideas filled the room. The Board Members had nicknames for each other borrowing from the Ancient Greeks. One was 'Birdbrainicus' - Ancient Greek Nitwit. The second was 'Articules' - The Verbally Resplendent, and the third was 'Hideocritus' - Philosopher specializing in hideous mediocrity. Together they had come up with some wacky ideas over the years. Their answering machine at the reception desk said, "We have an 'outstanding' customer service department. They are 'out standing' on the front porch smoking cigarettes right now." The company succeeded in spite of itself. They were considered by their loyal customers as being way out on the edge. Their biggest sellers were "Bed-Head Wigs" and sweaters made from Yak hair. In one of the offices, a design manager named Ronnie Roadrash briefed his new secretary, Pixie Glert. "You are going to overhear things that you shouldn't, Pixie. Just remember, you're supposed to have a short memory, and don't forget it!" Pixie tossed her candy wrapper on the floor and dug her heel into it. Ronnie asked her to pick it up and Pixie replied, "Why do you think they call it refuse? Most people refuse to pick it up."

Vignette 6

At the local "early-bird" special in Greater Ache, Alabama the silence was deafening. You could hear the collective groaning and creaking of eyebrow hairs sprouting in reckless abandon from the patrons thereabout quietly dining. You could hear an occasional grunt or the clearing of someone's throat or someone saying "Huh?!" Many a tidbit of conversation was stopped cold by an ear canal heavily congested by a tangling of ear hair. All was not about pleasantries and the daily offerings of joy that retirement can sometimes bring, but oftentimes it was about the soup that was cold, the bread that was stale, or the waiter who apparently hadn't bathed. You could hear accusations of stinginess, slovenliness, and graft. There were toupees tilting and Jell-O chunks that had made the fateful, silent journey from fork to floor. One elderly gentleman, having heard too many details about his wife's incontinence prevention asked her, "Can we have serenity now, and talk about Serenity-Pads later?" Another couple at the bar was approached by a Jehovas Witness and asked, "Have you found God?" The wife answered grudgingly, "No, why? Is he missing?" It all came to a head when someone started to choke after ordering the latest orange juice derivative, "Nothing but Pulp". An attentive fry cook knew the Heimlich maneuver and came to the rescue. When the pulp was violently expelled, and the excitement finally subsided, the early-bird crowd filtered out through the front door into the glaring sun with their gigantic wrap-around sunglasses to live another day.

Vignette 7

A busload of tourists had gone to Memphis for the Graceland tour. The usual introductions were taking place as the tourists mingled out front. "Hi, were from Wisconsin. I'm the big cheese", said one man. The guide started the tour in the kitchen, "In this freezer is a half-eaten ice cream Sunday from Elvis and Priscilla's first date." It was all very fascinating to some, especially a local realtor lady who told how she used to trick-or-treat in the neighborhood. A government nuclear facility that processed plutonium had been operating there when she was young. She suspected that that was the reason she could never have children. She had tried to sue the Government, but gave up. "It's better to be barren and sterile than starin' down a barrel", she said. It was a clear reference to Government intimidation. Gravitational pull had gotten the best of her. The gleaming gold ornamental bicuspids that she had recently purchased were her most noticeable beauty upgrade. As she was leaving, they all waved goodbye to her and her dog Pomeroy. As her car pulled out, it back-fired. Everyone dove for cover. She stuck her head out the window laughing and shouted, "It gets me where I want to go, I'd better keep it." As she drove away, a bumper sticker clearly read "Dog is my co-pilot."

Vignette 8

Down at the local police station a guy was being interrogated. He described a getaway car to police as "a powder blue Daewoo Legauza CDX 2003 luxury edition."

The interrogation team realized that only the actual owner would know a car description in that much detail. They cuffed him with complete confidence that they had their man. Even if they were wrong, they felt that anyone who would own such a car should be arrested anyway on general principals. Either way, that was Memphis justice.

The owner of the Blue Daewoo, Gerber Sniffleberry, was a mailman who had been hoarding product samples rather than distributing them. A list of items found in the Daewoo were "Big Bang popcorn", "Tuba Toothpaste", "Biohermitage Hemp Dressing", " Pollywanna Crackers", "Captain Siamese-Twin Cereal", and "Starterchex" a crunchy new cereal for babies. It was more than the judge could bear, the local citizenry being deprived of the benefits of such fine new products. Gerber Sniffleberry was sentenced to six months on a different route in a neighborhood that had a high population of dogs. He traded the Daewoo for a Dodge "Rambo." It would give him the defensive edge and getaway power that would be required on his new route. One time he was getting chased down the sidewalk by a strange looking, rather large dog. It was either a Chihuaberman or a Great HuaHua. It was a mixed breed of Great Dane and Chihuahua. Whatever it was, Gerber ran like hell to his Dodge Rambo to get away from the giant lumbering beast with the tiny head, all the while throwing his new samples of Barbie Tree-food spikes at the beast to hold it at bay or at least slow it down. He got into the car just as he nailed the dog with a bottle of Tubby McGumpkin's hair remover. The little Chihuahua head was stuck in the door. The stench of medieval dog food breath quickly filled the car. Gerber reached into his mailbag before passing out, pulled out the last Barbie Tree-food spike sample and knocked the

44

yapping freak dog unconscious. When he came to, the Great HuaHua was gone. Gerber crawled out of his car and completed his route. Mr. Sniffleberry later went on to start the "Let's Breed Sanely" foundation for dogs.

Vignette 9
Down on the South side, Hugh Manatee was attentively viewing a new movie, "Crouching Grandma, Terrified Child" after having just finished watching "Silence of the Clams" and "Jurassic Pork", when into the room wandered his friend, "Cape-Wearing Man", a neighbor who would pop in, at first intimating that he was there to stop some sort of crime, but then pausing as if he weren't sure why he was dressed as a Super-Hero in the first place. This went on for months until one day Cape-Wearing Man was walking down Main Street and the alarm bells went off at the bank across the street. It was at this point that the true nature of Cape-Wearing Man's valor became painfully apparent. He looked straight forward, started whistling a tune, as if oblivious to the bank heist occurring in his midst, and at his first opportunity, darted around a corner and disappeared.

Vignette 10
Upon boarding the new "Reality Airways", Heather Liplock, in her first official flight as a stewardess, couldn't help but notice the immediate sensation of being coughed on as passengers boarded the plane, and feeling nauseated by the sound of people clearing their throats. She had been briefed on this phenomenon during training and had received commendations from the directors of the fledgling airline for providing the impetus to implement a novel approach to the phlegm problem. Heather

announced with precise hand signals so that she would be clearly understood, "Please fasten your seat belts after you have settled in. There is a 'throat clearing' area at the back of the plane. We strongly suggest that you take advantage of this opportunity to clear your throat. Anyone who is entertaining the idea of coughing up phlegm for the next three hours must understand that Reality Airways does not consider this to be a realistic option. Making noises with offensive phlegm and spreading germs is not permitted on any Reality Airways flight. We serve pretzels in bulk from a fifty pound box to help keep our fares as low as possible. Single serving wrappers have been discontinued to reduce our carbon footprint. Also, we highly encourage well-timed courtesy flushing. So sit back and enjoy some peace, quiet and fresh air on Reality Airways where, when it comes to our passenger's comfort, the sky's the limit."

Vignette 11

The peace of the morning was shattered by the sound of my neighbor's chainsaw. A disturbing gastric state wasn't helping much. I had tripped over a chunk of road kill and sprained my ankle the day before and had not been keeping up with my nose hair maintenance program. Bizarre neck and shoulder hair were hampering me even further. All that being said, my girlfriend Pixie yelled up from downstairs, "Honey, the coffees ready and the kitchens clean, you can come down now." She had called into work to tell her boss she was taking a vacation day. Pixie had a PHD in Pseudoscience. We were both living off the fumes of a rosier past and had come to an uneasy truce with our ambitions. We even got library cards just so we could go in and 'SHOOSH' people. We had five pounds of coupons, and a little money, as we headed for the store, hoping for the best. Our SUV, the Grand Larvae, looked like a giant grubworm on wheels. It wasn't very aerodynamic, but it would float if we should ever happen to drive into water. We got in and headed down the highway. In the awkwardness of the moment, we both glimpsed a brief look into the rear-view mirror. Who needs a rear view mirror when you're going a 100 m.p.h. in a car that looks like a grubworm? Who would want to stop us? That's how we made it through life. We tried to have a few laughs everyday and things usually worked out. We got off the highway and pulled into the Quickie Mart. We smelled of Crunchy Cheetos and Redbull, but who would notice? Behind us in line was an overly jealous wife who was getting mad at her husband for trimming his nose hair earlier that morning. "Who were you getting prettied up for?" she demanded. We were trying to get to Reptile World for vacation. Pixie was wearing out her blinkers and her tires making too many wrong turns. When the rims finally hit the road, we screeched to a halt. We sat and waited for the wheel to cool down so that we could change the tire. Fortunately, our spare had a little tread left on it. There were a few vultures lurking around because some escaped reptiles had been hit by cars. An iguana watched me intently as I changed the tire. We were very hungry and couldn't wait to get home to have some Panko Encrusted Tuna Helper. The horizon moment came as we were driving into our home town. We noticed a new business. The sign said "Over and Dunwith Funeral Home." It reminded us of how short life is. We held hands and renewed our vows that we would stay together until death does its part.

Chapter 5
Poems

Freedom is a walk
Alone along the beach
Freedom is hearing
The sound of your own speech
Freedom is a gift
Paid with struggles long
Freedom is the wind
Carrying a song

Somewhere in the world
A truly solemn scene
Windswept, is unfurled
From a barely awakened dream

_____

There is sanctuary in places
Where you keep pictures of the heart
Where you look before you leap
Where God is the sky
Lightning, a blinking eye
Crickets, a lullaby
And rain, the eraser of pain

_____

To the rushing
We're a void
At the crushing
We're annoyed
As a race

We've lost control
At our dying
Wander souls
By the street
A cold kid stares
At his feet
While no one cares

On the simmering paths
We seek the shade
And rest our heads
Upon the leaves

For the child we make
A bed is laid
For them to sleep
So we can gaze
At the innocence
We long to keep

———————————

Chasing sunshine
Drinking rains of spring
Bare trees comb the winds
As they whisper
And they sing
Waking to the thaw
And the squirrels claw
Earth is breathing wild again
Colors fill the day
People lost in play
As Heaven ships
And ghostly flashes
Drift on the air

Earth holds fast
As night rolls on

Flowers close
And the night becomes
A rolling shadow
Of the stars

The tracks of broken tears
Bonds of ice silenced
Cold and crushed
On vacant rail

Ambling over cobblestones
Old brick buildings lean and moan
Carriage wheels and ghost-like steam
In a barely-awakened dream

The Rock House, full of
Damp, Dusty Spiders
That weave in a web museum
Hesitantly take a path
Of forced containment
Where the empty chair still rocks
The spiders were made to hide
The cold, lonely stone
Became the warmth of home
Their ghost house
Is open to familiar haunts
But the ghosts
Have all been and gone

The long unwoken dreams

Haunt what's left
Of a country mansion
As the wind sways
The cold cracking timbers
Stricken icicles, barely melted
Fall away
Thawing what's left
Of the frozen hearth within

Like tin lizards
We grope
High on skies
Of smoldering hope
Equating ideals
To extinct kingdoms
Busily not remembering
Refuge among picket fences

There's a fallen angel mending wings
Clipped by heathens and angry Kings
Pleading that we stand yet straighter
Amidst the fallen rows

All hail, as angels wake
An eagle perched in a tall tree
On a desolate beach
Peering into the distance
As if the peering matters
Or the distance can be reached

The Dandelion

Dormant, left in fallow ground
I lay for a year without a sound
Life stirs around this stage, this place
I have no name, I have no face
Only the ample chore from a given space

Drawn to see my place in the sun
Strewn by stars that churn the wind
Drowsily, I break through
Time has formed a dandelion

Some brothers and sisters were turned into wine
I was left to grow old and go to seed
I feel life leave me, the wind it blows
Dyin' like a dandelion, that's the way it goes

———————————

We are all ancient
Living a future dream
Send me history
Please sign me in
Find a way
Out of every storm
Keep in tune
Like the tide and moon
We paint our worlds
With different colors
Fly our flags
On separate winds
Attract ourselves
To fine ambitions
And in the morning
Start again

Rented friends
Make no amends
They channel ill advice
Their answers waft like pollen
And subside like the morning frost

True love is timeless
Consuming each instant
It is never mindless
It perpetuates kindness
True love respects
It is not demanding
And inspires those who are near

Lyrics for "City Street"-Chicago, 1977
On that city street there seemed to be
Someone who appeared in a long ago dream
Silhouettes in darkness, could be anyone
Is this dream at end, or has it just begun?
Pages of love, torn from time
Never remembering why
Familiar scattered scenes go by
I reach for the dream, I'm denied
Faces keep changing, can't find
What we're looking for
Like a hall with a million doors
And a chain with a million keys
Pages of love, torn from time
Never remembering why
Familiar scattered scenes go by
I reach for the dream, I'm denied
Faces keep changing, disguised

We look so much the same
Down to the hidden pain
Pages of love, torn from time
Never remembering why
Familiar scattered scenes go by
I reach for the dream, I'm denied
Lonely ...City Street
Lonely... City street
No shadows in the night
New illusions

_____

We've seen the thousand shields clashing
The gravel tombstones
And the indescribable degree of fraying
In the cold embrace of natures will

All the million stars that tried
Had no chance and so they died
Endless stars that keep on giving
Forever dreams that we are living

There's a ghost
Writing spaceship anthems
Drifting with the stars
Floating between emptiness
Outside of all

_____

All the proud and the lonely
All the same they wake
Forlorn amidst endeavors
Vying with the silence
In the shifting stills
Of windswept blue and gray

Skywhale (written at 30,000 ft.)
Skywhale, the heaving cloud
Laying sleek
Just below the heavens
The bringer of rain, it scoots
Like greased lightning
The creature stirs
For all life to heed
The ephemeral buoyant captivation
Slips through the rubble's claw
Drifting creatures
Like cloud frogs
Destined for transformation
The earth holds fast
Its fertile yawn
Through the drowsy night
Glancing at the skirted
Brow of eternity
While the myriad of humanity
Cradled in manicured realities
Tested by fathomless directors
Endure the cosmic writhing drama
Finite specks on this orbiting egg
We drift, not knowing if we matter
Or if we have become divine
In the unfolding mystery of life

To the wrecks of our elders
Ships laden with dreams
Shift idly on sands
And well rotting beams

Finite echoes
Of fading delirium
Rest upon
The hallowed sand

Torrid torment gently thrashing
At heartstrings
Longing for home

Bury me at Sea
So my bones wash up
As sand upon the beach

_____

Unwritten stories
Pageless moments
Your fondest memories
Priceless days in our lives
Reeling in heavens shallows
Parting shadows we have been
Weaving through sleepless limbo

_____

Countless years
Have come and gone
Since the spirit
Shone at dawn
And from his conscience
Man withdrew
Now all will gather
To face the truth
What was faith
Will remain such
But many souls
Will feel this touch

We who are here
Assemble so
For reasons we
May never know, yet
The sleeping pleas
Of times disease
Are stunned
To wake unanswered

Life is history
Passing like a freight train
Life is a swamp out gassing
Life is a subtle pain
Life is social
Life can be cruel
Life is a duel
Life is one big intersecting detail
An ant on a heap
A bee in a palm
A sloth half asleep
Your mom
Life is a chase
Life is a design
Life has a pace
Life has a mind
A turtle in a pond
A fish at the shore
A bleach blonde
And more
Life is a blink
Life is endless fishing
Sometimes it stinks
And seems to have no mission

A bird in a bath
A monkey in a zoo
A man in space
Me and you
Life is a trial
Life is a fright
We can freeze in the darkness
Or bathe in the light

Ode to Mary McDoogle
Little old Mary McDoogle, who suffered with sore feet
Bought herself a bicycle, with an extra cushy seat

She peddles it to and fro, always with great ease
McDooglin' every day, anywhere she might please

She's McDooglin' here and McDooglin' there
She's McDooglin' just about everywhere

She really loves to McDoogle, McDooglin' all over town
You might glimpse her race down the alley, or when she's
turning around

When it comes to McDooglin', she's certainly the best
When she's not out McDooglin', she's home getting some
rest

But she'll be right back out, McDooglin' real soon
Peddling strong and silent, under a sultry summer Moon

All I see is her flashing knees, and her visor all askew
McDooglin' around in circles, with nothing at all to do

If she's not McDooglin' now, she'll surely McDoogle soon
If you're lucky you might hear her whistle a McDoogle
tune

I see her in the park, and I see her on the street
McDooglin' all around, in the sweltering summer heat

She'll cross in front of traffic, not even a second glance
I sometimes think she's out, McDooglin' in a trance

She's been known to knock down strangers, on the
sidewalk for a stroll
I tell you all this McDooglin', will surely take its toll

She'll cut you off in traffic, you'll think she is quite mean
It's as if she is protected, by a shield that can't be seen

Mary McDoogle met her match, early one Saturday morn
McDooglin' across the traffic, she didn't hear the horn

Apparently Mrs. McDoogle, was not too good at hearing
Her vision also suffered, as the Mack truck was nearing

The Mack truck driver tried his best, to come to a stop, but
still
She took an unfortunate bounce, off his shiny Mack truck
grill

They photographed her side by side, with her McDooglin'
machine
Which was severely bent and twisted, and had completely
lost its sheen

The moral of this story, if one can be extracted
Is not to act the same way that Mary McDoogle acted

Please look both ways before a crossing, her actions do not repeat
For it won't be long, before you're hurtling along
On Mary McDoogle street.

To Vladimir Putin
You made a withdrawal
From your bank of pains
The fog of mental bondage
Eyeing vast cold circles

You braided arteries in your heart
Used hemostats to stop your tears
You reached out your hand of fate
Descending a long stairwell
You bade farewell

You are the drop of blood
Falling from a thorn
Causing a ripple
In a pool once clear

You are one face
In the light of a frozen shadow
While millions of faces flicker
Against the light of a fading sun

Your stone majesty is cracking

Under pure times rage
Your lost anthem ships and their fateful seeings are
Obscuring desperation and tribal groans

In your heart, replete with squandered wisdom
You advance like an ancient heathen
Bent on destruction
Yet considering no apology
Equating your ideals
To extinct kingdoms and
Withering atop ancient laurels

Like a dead star
Whose light we only now see
We never question the delay
But only long to feel
The dead warmth of you
The passing Son

Such is life
The wasted fragments of weathered time
Fettered by useless blame
Treading calamity upon cradled bliss
Always in search of a lasting moment

In the last fraudulent moment
Of planetary espionage
A bulbous oil glutton,
You maintain your slimy stance

Will you regret your greed
To give the globe just one more chance?
Will you die by the sword,

Or leap into a bullet?
Will you fight like a man,
Or flop like a mullet?
Could a worm after rain
On hard hot clay
Wriggle in its madness
To live another day?

Always starting over
Facing the wind
Salivating hungrily
At every whim
And it always seems to follow
We imagine wars and ruin

The idols of ruin
Keep playing along
Dusting their memories
And getting it wrong

A soul smashing clown
You leave the world bewildered
With horrific nonsense and Stupocracy
Heir apparent to a misguided dream
While you outrun the authorities

With no moral compass evident
And being essentially dead from the neck up
Lashing out sub-cerebrally
And doubling down on ignorance
In order to save face
It's your low regard for what obscures
Your vision that's befuddling

In your political dealings
We're not sure what card is being played
But it's not recognized as being from a full deck
Being unruly at best
Your complete disdain for anything
Remotely resembling human decency
Has become painfully evident

Having nothing but mean bones in your body
You couldn't pass a sniff test
Because all you do is stink

A pawning politician
Who became a crime
You ring the stolen bell
You rent existence
And pray to hell

And so it seems
As if the good things
The world has done
Can be lost

In counted hours
On stricken soil
Time will tell
As it tells all
Who will rise
And who will fall
Your severed ties
And useless blame
Are clever lies

They're all the same

And after all the brows were beaten
And every sages wisdom eaten
There were crows of illness
Fluttering in the stillness

_____

<u>Chapter 6</u>
The One-Liners

Just because great minds think alike doesn't mean that
people who think alike have great minds

With amoebic foresight we glimpse the future

You can't teach an old Gnu dog tricks

We're all geniuses until convinced otherwise

Words are engines that can guide us to great wealth or
misfortune

There's nothing better for thee, than someone else

If you cannot see what's coming, you'll never know
what hit you

Sin is: People who have it good, yet they still complain

I can fix machines, I can't fix people

Think outside the box…What box?

The threshold of dignity that we uphold will directly affect our standard of living

State Trooper to traveler: "Welcome to Georgia, here's your speeding ticket"

He could forget like there was no tomorrow

Advanced Hieroglyphics Encryption: How the Engineers who designed the Great Pyramids hide their mathematical formulas

There aren't any universal answers, only forcefully applied conclusions

Duct tape and determination is what got us to the moon and brought us back from the moon. If you want to go to the moon, you better take duct tape

Man and wife who own HUMVEE's: Their favorite thing to do is to fill up their gas tanks on Saturday night

As bored as a mollusk at dancing school

Don't let your ego outperform you

Never eat cotton candy in the rain

Daughter to Mom: "Why are people tossing cigarette butts out of their car window onto the streets?" Mom to daughter: "They don't want those disgusting things smelling up their car!"

Being of modest means growing up, I only had a Mr. Potato Head with an eye missing

The "Inaction Figures": Stunned, Amazed, Shocked, and Dismayed.

One plastic surgery patient to another: "Gladys had a nose once, but she blew it!"

Antiques Road Show: Person freaks out because the appraisal is too low on his Goat Hair Turkoman Fiesta Hat with Plumes. He has to be quickly escorted off the set

New show: "Sheep Watch" - Surveillance camera watching sheep in pasture, waiting to see if a wolf will attack one of them. The show has no redeeming value but everyone's watching it just because it's on T.V.

I called her and she never called me back. Now that's uncalled for!

"Numb and numb-er": The story of barbiturate addicts

Advertising campaign for Dentists: Put your money where your mouth is

There is a sinister plague upon Earth. It's called 'bad behavior'

Bumper sticker from God: Don't make me come down there!

Houdini Chicken: It's so delicious that it disappears before it even gets to the table!

Drug ad on TV: If you develop the inability to multiply by 7, have chronic halitosis, a persistent or unstoppable urge to play "Chutes and Ladders", stop taking SQLORNK if you experience any of these symptoms.

Trying to deal with Vladimir Putin is like blowing your nose into cheesecloth

Puritanically Tyrannical: Putin's insane ideological mental contortion

Film short: "Count Spatula" - Working at all-night diner flipping burgers. (A play on Dracula who can only work at night)

Realtor: "Any bites on your house?" Homeowner: "Yes, a grizzly was here last night and bit off the front porch!"

Song lyrics: Her boots are made for walking, but tomorrow she'll use 'em to cook, before you taste that soup, you'd better take a closer look.

Dinner prayer: "We got beans, we got franks, and for that, we give thee thanks"

They left the front, but they'll be right back.

The Rat Race has lost its allure

Cosmetic Surgery Center: Botox injections being given - In the afterglow of anesthesia a customer mumbles, "One more and I gotta go."

Alfred the Butler offering a breakfast of Robin Egg Omelet and Bat Fondue to Batman and Robin. They tactfully refuse.

The reason people don't stay on diets is because it gets in the way of their eating

I could give a rat's ass, but I'm not currently in possession of one

The frugal life: Knowing which cheap wine to buy

Misprinted sympathy greeting card: "Get real soon"

That was yesterday's spilled milk...let's move on

Thoughts people have, why they think they had them, and what they think of those thoughts now

A person who is totally wrong about something is usually the last one to know

New band: The Idle Pranksters

Hollywood Catholic confession: Priest tells actor to watch five 'Leave it to Beaver's', one 'Bonanza', and three 'Highway to Heaven's'

Profundities are the opposite of saying too much

Humans require too large a taste for oblivion

Knee slapping pad: For those hilarious family get-togethers

The only peace and quiet I get is the peace and quiet I make

Sorry, the cat's out of the bag but it was claustrophobic to begin with

You just may have to face what you may not feel like facing

That which makes you angry controls you

Milk of Amnesia: Take it and forget about it

Busier than a one-handed court reporter

Cloning has gone too far when the nightly news is introduced: "Tonight, sitting in for Norah O'Donnell is Norah O'Donnell."

Primadonna: Someone who refuses to use the same Kleenex twice

"Hello, did I wake you up?"… "No?"… "Well, go to sleep and I'll call you back."

Obsane = Obscene and Insane

Leaf blower guy: Wind blowing leaves right
back at him. Guess he can't afford to buy a rake

Nutcase gift recipient: "Wow, what a nutcase!"

It was either Socrates or Fred Astaire who said, "The
cutting in is easy, it's the dancing that's difficult.

Hideocrity = Hideous Mediocrity

Price is Right host: "I said, come on down, not take a
lap around the whole studio!"

The Gladys Kravitz Principal: Peek out the
window at your neighbors and hope that they
don't see you

Hollow commitment: When she told her new
boyfriend one night that she didn't feel like
pricing ham, that's when they decided to break up

9 out of 10 dentists prefer children who chew sugared
gum

Jungle native leaves his hut with usual tribal
dress, briefcase and a businessman's hat. He says
goodbye to wife. Gets to his hut of business,
flips a sign over that says "Sorry, We're Open."
Opens briefcase containing voodoo dolls.

Man on hands and knees lunging toward
scattering marbles. They go down a sewer grate.
"This time Sam Melvin really lost his marbles."

A possessed dust buster: You can hear it
vacuuming in the middle of the night

Light Whitening: New moonshine flavored
toothpaste

Skit: Guy and girl at drive-in movie. Guy asks
girl if she wants to get in the back seat. She says
"No, I want to stay up here with you."

Technology has gone too far when an 8-year-old trick-
or-treating ghost is busy talking on his cell phone
complaining to his Mom about the low quality of treats.

A kid, preparing for a spelling bee, spelled
"antidisestablishmentarianism" in his alphabet
soup yesterday

Sign in store window: "No shirts, No shoes, No
service." There was a naked lady behind the
counter. I asked her for an ice-cream cone and
she didn't respond. The sign was accurate!

Struggling Fraternity: Halfa Cuppa Tuna

New sporting event at the Dust Bowl: Tumbleweed
Soccer

Johnny's report card says he excels in Foul Languages

She had phenomenal candor

There's a big difference between "You have to see it to believe it" and "You have to believe it to see it." i.e. Seeing the Virgin Mary's face on a piece of toast

Girl trying to shoplift two rolling suitcases: Security man taps her on the shoulder as she approaches the exit. "Where do you think you're going? She replies innocently, "Acapulco, then Prague." Security guard tells her to have a nice trip.

Soap Opera: As the Sap Flows

New band: The Vain Ogres

Sign on Birdbath during drought: <u>5 Second Drinks Only</u>

Why don't they call it B.O.derant?

Some people are looking for work and hoping to God not to find it

Incandeathsentence light bulbs: The original light bulb that should have been phased out over a century ago

High-minded riff-raff: They were last seen eating caviar off of paper plates and smoking cigarettes in front of the pawn shop

There are people out on the road doing everything in

their car <u>except</u> driving

It seems these days that even the vultures are getting lazy. I've been passing the same dead raccoon everyday for about a week now

Don't waste time thinking about how much time you're wasting.

We're a spectacle of atoms, twinkling in our own imaginations

No matter where we are, we have arrived at our destination

Everything we do tweaks the fabric of the space-time continuum

Last time I checked, we were all in the same boat

If you view the Earth as a grain of sand in a sea of space, you will find that there is little demand for big egos

Space awaits us, as Earth did our birth. The womb is unending

We are chemistry, we like symmetry

I could tell you a thing or two around three

Get rid of time, pennies, nose hair and anything else that doesn't make any sense

Who cares about a car's horsepower? The speed limit is 70mph

Half Blessing and Half Curse = BLURSE

Even if it seems we're just moving sideways, we have to keep moving

An incessant twinge of exasperation

Some people are working hard at hardly working

It's so hot and dry that cowchips are randomly detonating and people are buying Teflon bedsheets

The L.C.D. (lowest common denominator) syndrome is engulfing American society

I just squinted and saw a "No Golfing" sign on the moon!

Goofing and Golfing a Round seem too similar to dismiss as a mere coincidence

When the sheer magnitude of the world in front of our eyes blurs into a sensation of overwhelming disbelief, that is when we might decide to think not so much about ourselves, but dwell on the greater good instead

Don't define yourself by your failures

Silence, left unchecked, becomes the servant of the loud

When the lights begin to flicker, you no longer need the switch

We should be able to count on our fellow human beings to feel empathy

Neural pathways are now being called into the service of something greater than our own egos

No one said what you leave behind has to be progeny

We don't all have to be experts

Change your consciousness, celebrate Nostril Awareness Month

After the parade of endless civilizations ceases, is the pile of reworked dreams half of what was meant to be?

Status quos have an expiration date

Clyde O'Scope: Irish Psychedelic Historian

Over-emoting is not a form of entertainment

The Demolition Derby at the County Fair was disappointing for one driver. He apparently forgot to disable the steering wheel airbag

No matter where you are, you are still directly above the center of the Earth

Don't let your mouth lead your mind

Phonezillas: People who spend most of their time looking at their phones

Embroidered on the back of some motorcycle riders jacket, it read 'Born to Break Wind'

People can overpopulate, but bugs do it better

We all keep coming up for air

There's no excuse for abuse

'Keeping up with the Jones' is a huge waste of time and energy. Everyone is *ahead* in some respects and *behind* in others

We can't out run fate. We can only share the race

Condo pet restriction: 'No Cyclops Terriers'

Try not to spend too much time looking in the rear view mirror

It's all fleeting...everything fleets

When we help others, we are also helping ourselves

You can only make the same 'honest mistake' once

We're either dragging each other through the mud or getting a ride in a rickshaw

Guns kill people, it's time for people to kill guns

I don't have the heart to save a cockroach

Sharon Sharalike: Voted most likeable student in School

Reality check: What's the point of having reality if you can't check it once in a while?

Breaking News vs. Non breaking news? It's all breaking news or it wouldn't _be_ news! It's really just newer news.

"Cy Clops…nice guy, you can really see eye to eye with him

When you can no longer see a halo around your head, you should start to feel better

Where the ice gets thin, we all fall in

Example of redundancy: 'Angry Mob'

The first one to smile in a room of angry people is deemed suspect

New Cooking Directions: 1. Pre-heat oven 2. Bake for 15 minutes 3. Don't over eat

Banks are now offering 'Free identity theft'

Keep looking for the light at the end of the tunnel. It's in there somewhere

Acceptance, Enjoyment, and Enthusiasm: That's all there is

In a crowd of dunces, I don't fare well

Something has to be the fulcrum upon which we rely to balance our destiny

If all we do is 'think', we cannot 'know'

The next light switch you flip might change the world forever

Woulda, Coulda, Shoulda...Didn't

Spellbound Dust Mites: Amazed at the power of Madge's new vacuum cleaner

We're not here to do the impossible

Our biggest fear should be ingrown hair

Wife: "When are you going to start listening?"...Husband: "I started listening to you an hour ago."

New Game Show: "The Miscellaneous Pots and Lids Show" where everyone is determined to match a pot with its proper lid. "Our 1st contestant is a house wife from Ogallala, Nebraska..."

Don't forget the remainder of your reminder

Make a reminder to remember the forget-me-nots

Guffawing at some vomitous retort by a 'Brand X' news caster, the depth of his shallowness became quite evident

My goal in life was to return all her Tupperware intact with matching lids

There are fools for trying and fools for not trying

Socially sidewardly mobile

A new clothing line: "Remember Wear" - One size fits all

She was hug challenged: She didn't know whether to hug left or hug right

Snug as a bug in a rug: A lobster napping in a toupee

Gregarian chants: Humans synchronizing the universal harmonic balancing process in one friendly chant

Valentine's Day card: "I'm trying to get a lot of things out of my hair, and you're not one of them. Happy Valentine's Day!"

The whole point of listening is that you may never hear it again

The question is: What is the question?

No one has ever answered the question, "What is the point?"

With machinery, you have to be able to sense when the machine no longer wants fixing

Put one foot in front of the other and you'll get to the end of the line

Crying will only get you as far as the next tissue box

Some people are too busy being attached to their possessions

Hairtrigger, USA: Where there are more guns than people

If we are living in the moment, we won't be needing to take many photographs

In the race through life, if you're going to run the red lights, please look both ways first

Truck driver from Port-O-Let: Talking shit on his cell phone

Good Salesman: He could talk a dog off a meat truck

Once you start spilling it, you should stop drinking it

I'm not here to pass along genes

One last roach sprang forth as the asteroid hit

Discount Circus: The big attraction is a Stripeless Zebra

I got a meat and potatoes job for Tofu wages

Things change. That's the way it is...for a while

A worn out welcome is worse than a locked door

Keep putting one foot in front of the other in the hope that you don't find yourself moonwalking

Life starts today, try not to miss it

We're all just kicking the bucket down the road. Apparently, the can wasn't enough

Everyone has their own personal Twilight Zone

The more I thought of the idea, the less I thought of it

Let the ink dry before you turn the page

Mid Evolutionary conundrum: Humanity is simply not evolved enough to avoid destroying itself

Slow Horrendous Whiplash: The neck injury received the first time one witnesses Godzilla 'Dumpster Diving'

Focus on a void: The only way to quiet the mind

The art of noticing: Acknowledging others efforts

Live well, live often

We're all flesh, bones, and mistakes

Simply jaded: The history of the human race

Groomed for successive failures: Not getting proper attention or support during our formative years

The Identical Hairdo Family Singers

Curbside manners: People politely competing to get a taxi cab in New York City

Surgeons practice? - Don't practice on me!

Sergio Vendetta: Makes ill fitting jeans just for spite

Unemployed rubber-necker: Nothing new to look at

Pyroclastic Hootenanny: It might not be the safest party to attend

High roller: Throws dice over the entire craps table

Bleak Orbit: The story of space junk

Realidue = Reality + Residue

The Flattened Earth Society: The founder, Vladimir Putin, was later referred for treatment to I.C.B.A.P., the Intercontinental Birdbrain Assistance Program

Sense of shallow foreboding: Fairly certain that something is amiss

Theresay instead of Heresay: "Somebody said it over there."

Drink Heist: Guy grabbing any unattended drink at the party

Startling Embrace: When people you don't know suddenly give you a hug

Egregious falseisms abound: When every statement that comes out of somebody's mouth is a lie

The Threadbare Coattails: What uninformed voters desperately grab onto to stay attached to their "leader

Shallow superiority: What an imbecilic leader exhibits a sense of

A sitting ovation: For an 'almost-great' performance

Predictable flotsam: The story of a Flip-Flop that floated from Haiti to Vero Beach

Emblematic overkill: Egocentric people who put their names on everything, like buildings

Queen Kong: Wife of the late King wearing yoga pants

Sagebrush salad: High in fiber

Bumper sticker: 'Save Hugh Manatee'

Therapeutic bird watching

Straitjackets Required: Sign on entrance door at Palm Beach fundraiser

Poetic cement: Stuck trying to come up with two words that rhyme

Lethargic overthought...Time to take a nap

Figments of delirium: What narcissistic tyrants seem to be experiencing

The brink of distinction: Almost getting your point across

Dollar Llama: Far East Discount Gift Shop and Meditation Center

Thoughts melt: Better write them down

Gentlemen Bum: He might be poor, but at least he's polite

Mundane Mega Funk: The feeling we have when we wake up and we know the world is in trouble

Purveyor of fundamentalist glee: Definition of an optimist

Transcendental thought barricade: When you can't quite come up with the words to express what you are thinking

Innuendo as a verifiable rumor: When people make outrageous insinuations and try to force them down people's throats

Beyond toxicity: The floating pile of plastic garbage in the Pacific Ocean

An amoebic catharsis: The time when amoebas decided to evolve

Brutal hat rack: Made out of Moose antlers

Eloquent Clown: Too smart to be a clown. He loses his Clown license

IQ Bullies: Parade their knowledge in a combative way

Troubled carnival worker: Stops the amusement ride so that you remain upside down long enough that all of the loose change falls out of your pockets and falls to the ground where he can easily pick it up

Overbearing Cupid: Gets way too involved in his efforts as a match maker

Sherpa hide out: On Mt. Everest it's the only place Sherpas can get any privacy

Clown Retirement Village: Where clowns learn to live without their make-up

Nimbly tossed venom: Carefully enunciated insults

Public Malaise: The public's indifference to the collective strife in the world

The Yahoo from Oahu

Twitching Eyeball Syndrome: Nervous reaction to staring at cell phones too long

Techno Rubble: The garbage leftover from the Technological Revolution

Squeaky Tombstone: "This thing is keeping me un-dead!"

Vanishing Valet - "Nice car Mister!" Car is never seen again

Avoid-dance: What relatives do to ignore each other without actually coming out and expressing their dislike for one another

Opposing factions used to draw a 'line in the sand' that shouldn't be crossed. Now they draw a line in the mud and hope there is a flood

Vague barriers: What we perceive as being courteous social distancing

Reciprocating antipathy: The downward spiral of indifference

Period of marginal frenzy: An artificially hyped-up celebration

As the audience dwindles: 1970's Rock Concert drum solo

A passion for idleness: Example of an oxymoron

Helen Highwater: She always seems to be stuck between a rock and a hard place

Not one to dawdle: The Sherpa who climbed Mt. Everest for the 36th time

The last attractive goiter: Tattooed to look like a Watermelon

Suspicious baggage: Clothes hanging out around the edges of a suitcase indicate an overly hasty departure

Foraging for expectations: Hoping someone will notice you

Blame throwing: For people who refuse to be held accountable for their mistakes

New band: The Numb Skulls

Beware of the ill-timed courtesy flush

Maniacles: Ancient Greek maniac

Compunction junction: Where remorse gets sorted out

The Yuck stream: Where a lot of television programming is found

Withstain = Withstand and Sustain

Ingots Barclay: Aspiring wannabe Palm Beach investment banker

Each day is yours to invent. We cannot all be Edison's

Desire within your means

Separated eventualities reminisce

I saw beyond the illusion of being hurt

Embalmed in success: Some people who were born with silver spoons in their mouths

King Kong Brand 'Atom Smashers'

Primate soliloquy: What is heard the first time a chimpanzee looks into a mirror

Why the theatrics when the acting is substandard?

Don't judge me on my misfortunes

No one is sensational until someone sensationalizes them

Octane Jane: Drag racer

Everything starts to make sense when we stop trying to make sense of everything

If you put all yours eggs in one basket, the more likely it is that some will crack

It's possible to be rich and poor at the same time

Some politicians have the "Edsels" of brains. Their ideas may seem good at the time, but are not well thought out

Over Millennia humans, in general, don't seem to learn or advance from their mistakes. Greed almost invariably prevails

The ultimate goal of all human endeavors should be to leave the Earth as it was before we messed it up

Happy is the dog with one leg up

If life isn't living, then it's merely existing

Turning a blind eye is not a disguise

The last one to win loses

Reconcile yourself with the dust

The road is no longer a shortcut if it's jammed with cars

Gold-zilla: The favorite idol of billionaires

Life is a gas, try to limit its flatulence

Don't look too hard. You might miss it

The island of Japan is now Godzilla proof

Tarantula Hide-a-key: The ultimate in home security

People just want somebody to listen to them

It's difficult to define reality because everything is constantly changing

Satisfied, the masses line up for their next dose of lies

Hollywood's 'Walk of Fame': Tourist's waddle by like penguins coddling their offspring

Don't over under-estimate

New Band: The Hip Monks

The Quietarium: Where you can pay to experience complete silence

You start life hoeing a row and you end life hoeing a row. The rest of your life is how well you keep the weeds down

We're basically lizards, advanced enough to drive cars

If we can't laugh at ourselves, all is certainly lost

Ambivalence is mental paralysis

Some people are just parked at the crossroads

If I know anything, I will let you know

It's the same for us all. We either understand what is reflected in our mirror, or we don't

The catalyst doesn't get credit for the end result

Sarcasm allows people to laugh for only about 2 seconds

We are merely signposts on Mortality Street

The caveman's first parking brake was a flat spot on the wheel

Hideous mediocrity is getting to be the norm

Most products are overrated because advertisers are seemingly incapable of being honest

Notworking vs. Networking: It's better to be networking than to be not working

There is a fine line between irresponsibility and wanton neglect

Success is not believing in yourself TOO much

One problem is that humans are not taking enough advice from the lower life forms

It could all mean nothing if you don't share it

What the world needs now is a non-violent downheavel

Every human is a mini-universe

Respect one another's failures

Skateboarder's Rest Home: Even in old age they still ride, albeit they have more accidents

A cave man went to pick up his date. He left after waiting forty-five minutes. She wouldn't go out until she shaved her legs, waxed her lip, brushed and flossed, primped and teased, plucked and dyed, gargled, manicured and pedicured. It was the beginning of the end for spontaneous interaction between men and women. It is a theory being bandied about in Anthropological circles as to why the Neanderthals went extinct.

People feel most alive while standing on a ledge

The best disappearing acts have gone unnoticed

Average boredom no longer satisfies the masses

Growing old should be just like growing up, only different

None of us volunteered to be here. Would that not make us all equal?

A half ounce of plutonium equals a ton of dismay

We are exploring the boundaries of human ignorance. Fine tuning ambivalence toward the status quo

Being too high on the hog looks pretty offal

Diffuse ambiguity: Nowhere Man's answer to everything

Wits End Pub: Last stop on the Stand-Up Comedy Tour

Cloning is inevitable because there may not be an enough smart people to run the world

Life is a symbiotic mess of conflicting necessities

With amoeba speed, we slowly see the future

Flabbergasted by the overwhelming simplicity of nothingness

The road to rags is paved with good intentions

Some may not understand, but that's perfectly understandable

Copies available at Amazon.com

Made in United States
North Haven, CT
06 January 2024